which makes you
come into our lives and quickly go. Some
with the passing whisper of their
upon. Some people
never the same.
which makes you happy. Follow your heart
come into our lives and quickly go. Some

ISBN 0-7683-2063-1
Text by Flavia and Lisa Weedn
Illustrations by Flavia Weedn
© Weedn Family Trust
www.flavia.com
All rights reserved

Published in 1999 by Cedco Publishing Company
100 Pelican Way, San Rafael, California 94901
For a free catalog of other Cedco® products, please write
to the address above, or visit our website: www.cedco.com

Printed in Hong Kong

No part of this book may be reproduced
in any manner without written permission
except in the case of reprints in the context of reviews.

The artwork for each picture is digitally mastered using acrylic on canvas.

With love and gratitude to those kindred spirits whose dedication, endless support, and talented hands made this book a reality —— Lisa Mansfield, Jane Portaluppi, Diana Musacchio, Tyler Tomblin, Jennie Sparrow, Solveig Chandler, Hui-Ying Ting-Bornfreund, Kim Gendreau and Annette Berlin.

The Wedding Celebration of

Other Flavia Books for Adults

Vows of Love: Wedding Guest Register
Across the Porch from God: Reflections of Gratitude
Across the Porch from God: A Gratitude Journal
To Take Away the Hurt: Insights to Healing
Heart and Soul: A Personal Tale of Love and Romance
Heaven and Earth: A Journal of Dreams and Awakenings
Blessings of Motherhood: A Journal of Love
Dear Little One: A Memory Book of Baby's First Year
Passages: A Woman's Personal Journey
Celebrations of Life: A Birthday and Anniversary Book
Kindred Spirits: An Illustrated Address Book

Flavia Books for Children

The Little Snow Bear
The Enchanted Tree
The Star Gift
The Elephant Prince
My Little One: Bedtime Magic for Baby's Sweet Dreams
I Feel Happy: A Bedtime Book of Feelings

A WEDDING JOURNAL AND PLANNER

Vows of Love

Flavia and Lisa Weedn
Illustrated by Flavia Weedn

Cedco Publishing Company • San Rafael, California

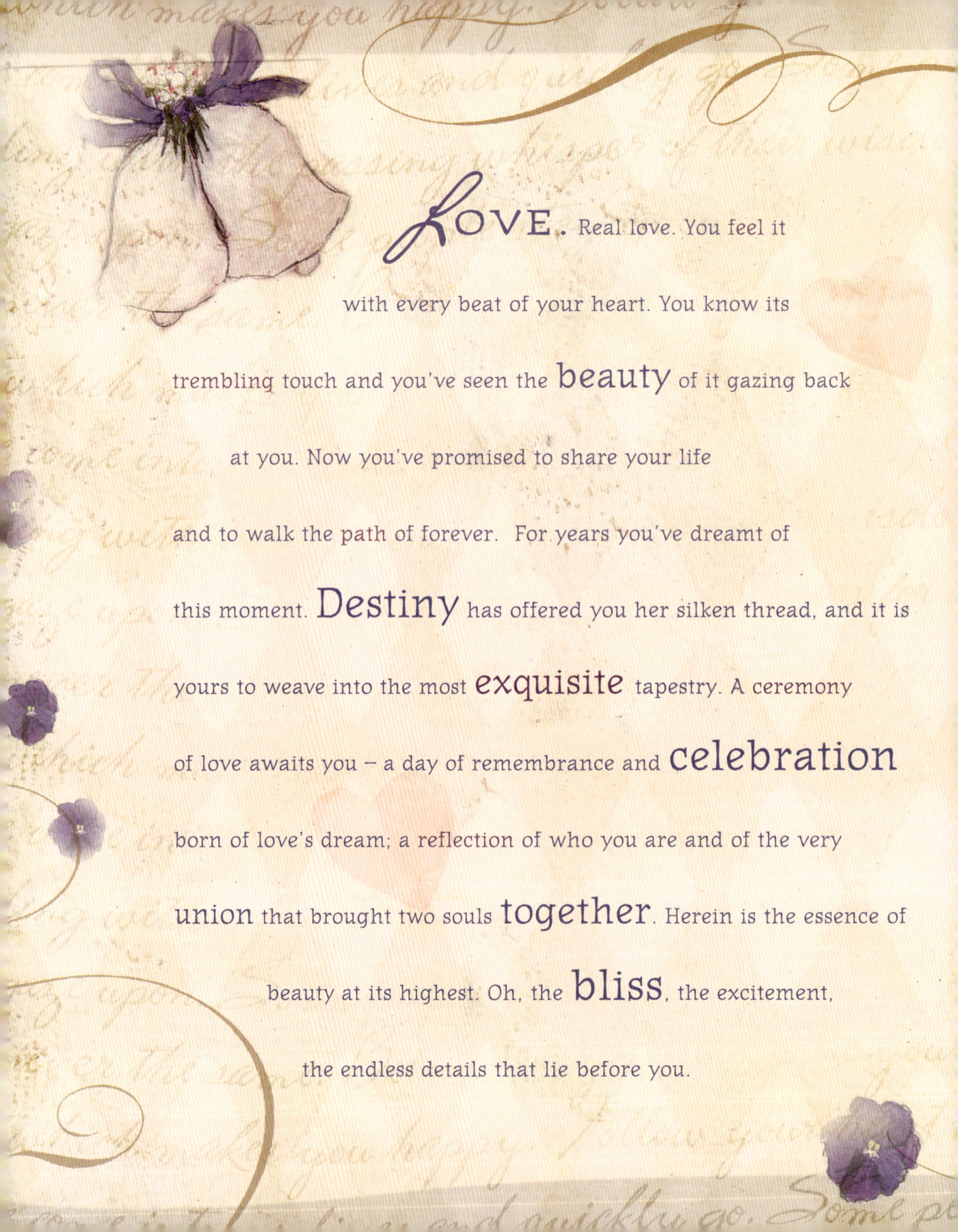

Love. Real love. You feel it with every beat of your heart. You know its trembling touch and you've seen the **beauty** of it gazing back at you. Now you've promised to share your life and to walk the path of forever. For years you've dreamt of this moment. **Destiny** has offered you her silken thread, and it is yours to weave into the most **exquisite** tapestry. A ceremony of love awaits you — a day of remembrance and **celebration** born of love's dream; a reflection of who you are and of the very **union** that brought two souls **together**. Herein is the essence of beauty at its highest. Oh, the **bliss**, the excitement, the endless details that lie before you.

Whether you're planning a large formal **wedding** or a small private **ceremony**, whether your tastes are traditional or unique in design, this journal and planner is designed to be your **companion** on the journey, helping to keep you organized and giving you room to record your private thoughts.

Be unafraid to **weave** each page with your dreams and **visions**.

Write poetry in the margins, or scribble down random thoughts of love and longing. Save clippings, fabric samples, pressed **flowers**, lyrics that **inspire**, and keep souvenirs of the **heart** safely wrapped within this book's embrace. Then tie them all in a satin ribbon and take **joy** – for these are the days you'll look back upon and cherish for all time.

Now and **forever**, may all that you **dream** of be yours.

Flavia

TABLE OF

Promising Forever

- The Proposal
- New Beginnings
- Blissful Hearts
- Tender Realities
- Sharing the News
- Blanket of Support

Visions & Reveries

- Love's Promise
- Defining Our Dream
- Love's Ritual
- Beautiful Imaginings
- Visions and Dreams
- Helping Hands

Weaving the Tapestry

- Threads of Time
- Turning the Hourglass
- The Ceremony
- The Officiate
- Our Vows
- The Wedding Party
- Silken Threads
- Satin Slippers
- A Shining Knight
- And His Men
- Beauty and Innocence
- A Family Affair
- Eternity's Embrace
- Remember Everything
- The Reception
- The Beauty of Flowers
- From the Garden
- Love's Music
- The First Dance
- The Food of Love
- Icing on the Cake

CONTENTS

Creating the Dream

Photography

Videography

The Honor of Your Presence

Keepsakes of the Heart

Guest Registry

Invitation List & Gifts Received

Details

Parties, Showers & Gifts

Sweet Anticipation

In Celebration

I Thee Wed

Time for Me

Private Moments

Loving Thoughts

Gifts of Heart

The Eve of Bliss

Our Wedding Day

Bride's & Groom's Recollections

Forever and Always

Cherished Memories

Souvenirs of the Heart

Paradise Found

The Honeymoon

On Our Way

His and Hers

Don't Forget

Remembrances

And Keepsakes

He took my hand,

I gazed into his SOUL;

an air of ancient beauty encircled us.

With quiet pauses,

trembling whispers,

and a lingering awareness

that all moments had

been leading us to this one,

we gave meaning

to FOREVER

with a single word

. . . YES.

Promising Forever

The Proposal

Remembering the Moment
_____
_____
_____
_____
_____
_____
_____
_____

When, Where & What Was Said
_____
_____
_____
_____
_____
_____
_____

New Beginnings

Engagement Ring

Setting the Date

Blissful Hearts

How We Felt
_____
_____
_____
_____
_____
_____
_____

Our Private Celebrations
_____
_____
_____
_____
_____
_____
_____

Tender Realities

Moments of Sharing

Remembrances

Sharing the News

Family Moments

Memories the Heart Will Hold

Blanket of Support

Our Circle of Friends

_____
_____
_____
_____
_____
_____
_____

Parties & Celebrations

_____
_____
_____
_____
_____
_____
_____
_____

When we open the door

to our **dreams**,

visions of the heart can

take us to **paradise**.

Heaven and Earth

meet in the reverie,

weaving the fanciful

thread of imaginings,

the texture of tradition,

and the **soulful** fabric of **devotion**

into the grace and fineness

of love's **celebration**.

Visions & Reveries

Love's Promise

What We Believe

Traditions We Honor

Defining Our Dream

First Discussions

Our Ideal Wedding Would Be

Love's Ritual

The Style of Ceremony & What We Visualize

Places We're Considering

Beautiful Imaginings

Poetry That Moves Us

Lyrics That Inspire

Visions and Dreams

Magazine Clippings, Color Schemes, etc.

Personal Notes

Helping Hands

Friends and Family

Wedding Consultant

WELCOME the lace and finery,

the satiny hues of color,

the fragrant petals and the

music of everlasting joy.

Revel in the promises to keep,

the LOVE to share

and all the moments leading up to the day

when two hearts

become ONE.

Weaving the Tapestry

Threads of Time

9-12 MONTHS AHEAD

Decide on Date, Style and Budget
Book Location for Ceremony
Book Location for Reception
Choose Wedding Party
Book Caterer
Book Florist
Book Photographer and Videographer

6 MONTHS AHEAD

Order Wedding Gown and Bridesmaids' Gowns
Order Shoes and Accessories for Bride and her Attendants
Book Musicians for Ceremony and Reception
Order Invitations and Other Stationery
Book Transportation/Wedding Cars
Make Honeymoon Plans

4 MONTHS AHEAD

Finalize Arrangements for Rehearsal Dinner
Book Accommodations for Wedding Party and Out-of-Town Guests
Discuss Availability of Flowers with Florist
Order Groom's and Groomsmen's Attire

3 MONTHS AHEAD

Finalize Guest List and Address Invitations
Required Blood Tests for Bride and Groom
Order Wedding Rings and Engraving
Arrange for Name Change on Official Documents
Finalize Decorations
Order Wedding Cake(s)

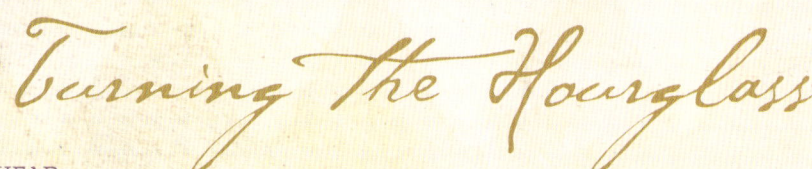

Turning the Hourglass

1 - 2 MONTHS AHEAD

Mail Invitations

Finalize Menu with Caterer

Finalize Ceremony Details and Music Selections

Purchase Gift for Spouse-to-Be

Purchase Gifts for Attendants and Family

Book Hair and Beauty Appointments

Purchase Lingerie for Wedding Outfit

Purchase Going-Away Outfit and Trousseau

Purchase Favors, Guest Book & Pen

2 WEEKS AHEAD

Bride and Groom Get Marriage License

Confirm Number of Guests Attending

Confirm Last Minute Details with All Vendors

Write Guest Place Cards for Reception

1 WEEK AHEAD

Finalize Seating Plan

Review Wedding Day Schedule

Confirm Processional/Recessional Sequence

Write a Love Letter to Your Spouse-to-Be

1 DAY BEFORE

Pamper Yourself with Hair and Beauty Treatments

Attend Rehearsal & Rehearsal Dinner

Give Spouse-to-Be Their Wedding Gift

WEDDING DAY

Take Joy !

The Ceremony

Location: ....
....

Contact: ....
....

Phone: ....
....

Fee: ....

Deposit Paid: ....

Balance Due: ....

Parking Arrangements: ....
....

Decorations: ....
....
....

Special Notes: ....
....
....

The Ceremony

Scheduling the Day:

The Officiate

Name: .... Phone: ....

Address: ....

Fee: .... Scheduled Meeting(s): ....

....

Preliminary Religious Requirements (if any): ....

Special Instructions: ....

....

....

(paste marriage certificate here)

Our Vows

Words of Love & Promises to Keep

The Wedding Party

Name:
Address: Phone:
Responsibilities:

Name:
Address: Phone:
Responsibilities:

Name:
Address: Phone:
Responsibilities:

Name:
Address: Phone:
Responsibilities:

Name:
Address: Phone:
Responsibilities:

Name:
Address: Phone:
Responsibilities:

The Wedding Party

Name:
Address: Phone:
Responsibilities:

Name:
Address: Phone:
Responsibilities:

Name:
Address: Phone:
Responsibilities:

Name:
Address: Phone:
Responsibilities:

Name:
Address: Phone:
Responsibilities:

Name:
Address: Phone:
Responsibilities:

Silken Threads

BRIDAL GOWN

Dress purchased at: ....

Contact: .... Phone: ....

Cost: .... Deposit Paid: .... Balance Due: ....

Date Ordered: .... Pick-up Date: ....

Fittings: ....

....

....

Special Notes: ....

....

....

Veil/Headpiece: ....

....

Shoes: ....

....

Lingerie and Accessories: ....

....

....

....

Satin Slippers

MAID OF HONOR & BRIDESMAIDS

Dresses purchased at:

Contact: .... Phone: ....

Cost: .... Deposit Paid: .... Balance Due: ....

Date Ordered: .... Pick-up Date: ....

Fittings:

Special Notes:

Shoes and Accessories:

A Shining Knight

GROOM'S ATTIRE

Outfit from:

Contact: Phone:

Cost: Deposit Paid: Balance Due:

Date Ordered: Pick-up Date:

Alterations/Fittings:

Shoes:

Accessories:

Items Ordered:

Special Notes:

And His Men

GROOMSMEN & USHERS

Outfits from:

Contact: Phone:

Cost: Deposit Paid: Balance Due:

Date Ordered: Pick-up Date:

Alterations/Fittings:

Shoes:

Accessories:

Items Ordered:

Special Notes:

Beauty and Innocence

FLOWER GIRL

Outfit from:

Contact: Phone:

Cost: Deposit Paid: Balance Due:

Date Ordered: Pick-up Date:

Fittings:

Shoes & Accessories:

Special Notes:

RING BEARER

Outfit from:

Contact: Phone:

Cost: Deposit Paid: Balance Due:

Date Ordered: Pick-up Date:

Fittings:

Shoes & Accessories:

Special Notes:

A Family Affair

PARENTS

Outfits from:

Contact: Phone:

Cost: Deposit Paid: Balance Due:

Date Ordered: Pick-up Date:

Fittings:

Shoes & Accessories:

Special Notes:

FAMILY MEMBERS

Outfits from:

Contact: Phone:

Cost: Deposit Paid: Balance Due:

Date Ordered: Pick-up Date:

Fittings:

Shoes & Accessories:

Special Notes:

Eternity's Embrace

WEDDING RINGS

Jeweler:

Contact: Phone:

Cost: Deposit Paid: Balance Due:

Date Ordered: Pick-up Date:

Sizes:

Engravings:

Special Notes:

(paste photos or sketches here)

Remember Everything

IMPORTANT THOUGHTS & NOTES

The Reception

Location :

Contact: Phone:

Fee: Deposit Paid: Balance Due:

Style Notes & Decorations:

Rentals (if not provided by Caterer) & Seating Arrangements:

The Reception

Scheduling the Day (Receiving Line, Cake Cutting, Etc.)

The Beauty of Flowers

FLOWERS FOR THE WEDDING PARTY

Florist:

Contact: Phone :

Total Cost: Deposit Paid: Balance Due :

Bride's Bouquet:

Maid of Honor's Bouquet:

Bridesmaids' Bouquets:

Flower Girl: Ring Bearer:

Groom's Boutonniere:

Groomsmen's Boutonnieres:

Mothers', Grandmothers', Sisters' Corsages:

Fathers', Grandfathers', Brothers' Boutonnieres:

Special Instructions and Delivery:

From the Garden

FLOWERS FOR THE CEREMONY

Total Cost: Delivery and Set-up:

FLOWERS FOR THE RECEPTION

Total Cost: Delivery and Set-up:

Love's Music

MUSIC FOR CEREMONY

Musicians:

Contact: Phone:

Fee: Deposit: Balance Due:

Set-up Arrival: Starting Time:

Music Requested:

Soloist or Special Songs:

Playing Schedule:

The First Dance

MUSIC FOR RECEPTION

Musicians: ....
....

Contact: .... Phone: ....

Fee: .... Deposit: .... Balance Due: ....
....

Set-up Arrival: .... Starting Time: ....

The First Dance: ....
....

Music Requested: ....
....
....
....
....

Playing Schedule: ....
....
....

The Food of Love

CATERER

Caterer/Restaurant:

Contact: Phone:

Number of Guests: Food Cost Per Person:

Number of Service Staff: Service Staff Cost Per Hour:

Set-up Arrival: Departure Time:

Menu:

Special Diet Request:

Beverages:

Icing on the Cake

THE WEDDING CAKE

Baker: ....

Contact: .... Phone: ....

Cost: .... Deposit Paid: .... Balance Due: ....

Description of Cake(s): ....
....
....

Decoration of Cake Table: ....
....
....
....

Delivery Instructions: ....
....
....
....
....

Special Notes: ....
....
....
....

Watch closely now,

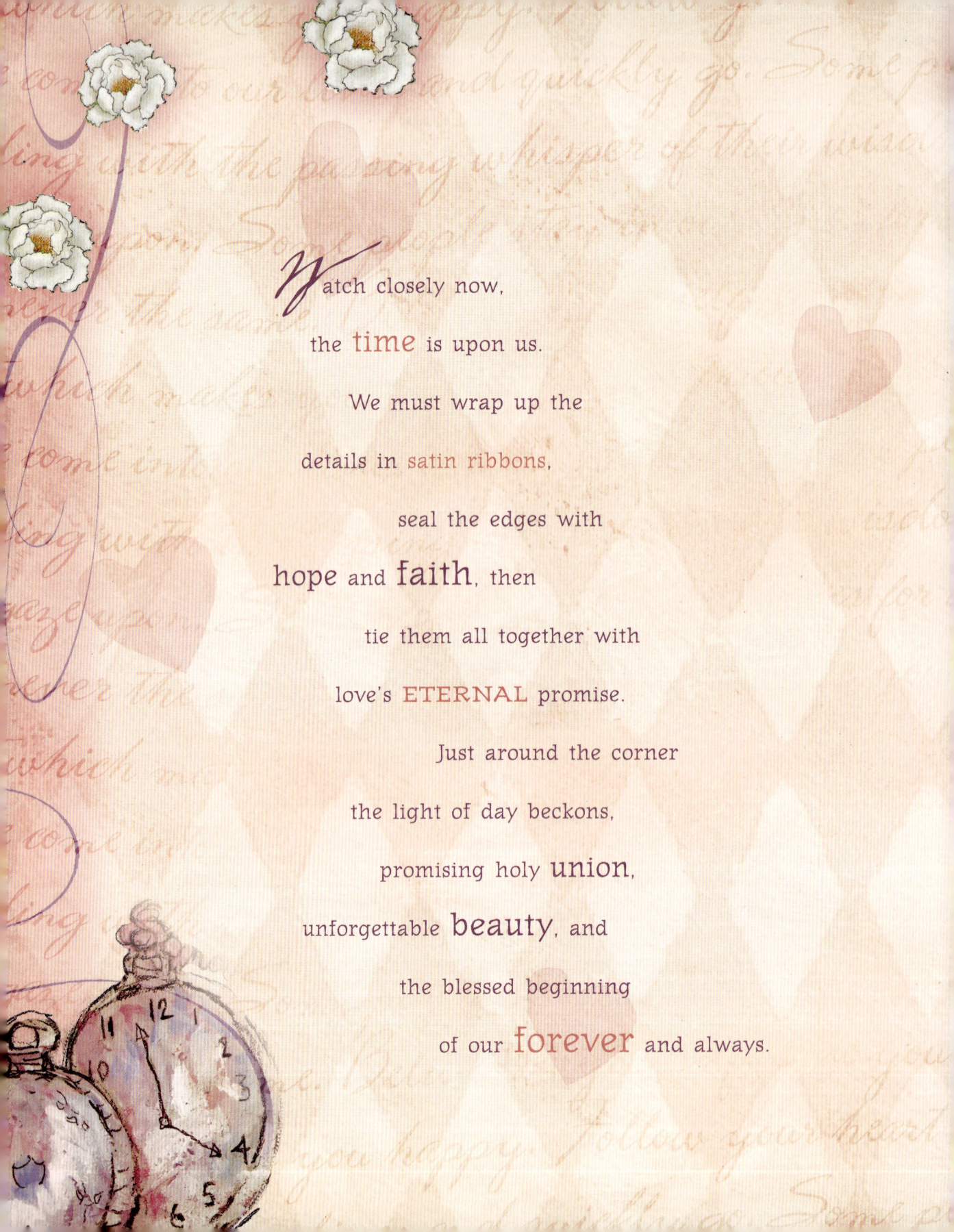

the time is upon us.

We must wrap up the

details in satin ribbons,

seal the edges with

hope and faith, then

tie them all together with

love's ETERNAL promise.

Just around the corner

the light of day beckons,

promising holy union,

unforgettable beauty, and

the blessed beginning

of our forever and always.

Creating the Dream

Photography

PRE-WEDDING PORTRAITS

Photographer: ....

Contact: .... Phone: ....

Fee: .... Deposit Paid: .... Balance Due: ....

Preferred Portrait Style: .... Where: ....

Appointment Schedule: ....

Photographs to Be Viewed: .... To Be Delivered: ....

WEDDING DAY PHOTOGRAPHS

Photographer: ....

Contact: .... Phone: ....

Fee: .... Deposit Paid: .... Balance Due: ....

Arrival Time: .... Departure Time: ....

Number of Prints/Slides: ....

Color / Black & White: ....

People, Events, Places to Photograph: ....
....

Reprints: ....

Albums for Bridal Couple: ....

Albums for Family: ....

Photographs to Be Viewed: .... To Be Delivered: ....

Videography

VIDEO SERVICES

Videographer:

Contact: Phone:

Fee: Deposit Paid: Balance Due:

Arrival Time: Departure Time:

Number of Tapes to Be Delivered: Date:

People, Events to Videotape:

Special Instructions:

The Honor of Your Presence

INVITATIONS

Stationer: ....

Contact: .... Phone: ....

Style of Invitation: ....

....

....

Text Chosen: ....

....

....

....

Quantity Ordered: .... Delivery Date: ....

Cost: .... Deposit Paid: .... Balance Due: ....

OTHER STATIONERY

....

....

....

....

Keepsakes of the Heart

TO REMEMBER

(paste sample of invitation here)

Gift Registry

Store:

Contact: Phone:

Registered for:

Store:

Contact: Phone:

Registered for:

Invitation List

Name & Address::
Phone: Number Attending:
Gift: Thank-You Sent:

Name & Address:
Phone: Number Attending:
Gift: Thank-You Sent:

Name & Address:
Phone: Number Attending:
Gift: Thank-You Sent:

Name & Address:
Phone: Number Attending:
Gift: Thank-You Sent:

Name & Address:
Phone: Number Attending:
Gift: Thank-You Sent:

Name & Address:
Phone: Number Attending:
Gift: Thank-You Sent:

Name & Address:
Phone: Number Attending:
Gift: Thank-You Sent:

Name & Address:
Phone: Number Attending:
Gift: Thank-You Sent:

Name & Address:
Phone: Number Attending:
Gift: Thank-You Sent:

Name & Address:

Phone: Number Attending:

Gift: Thank-You Sent:

Name & Address:

Phone: Number Attending:

Gift: Thank-You Sent:

Name & Address:

Phone: Number Attending:

Gift: Thank-You Sent:

Name & Address:

Phone: Number Attending:

Gift: Thank-You Sent:

Name & Address:

Phone: Number Attending:

Gift: Thank-You Sent:

Name & Address:

Phone: Number Attending:

Gift: Thank-You Sent:

Name & Address:

Phone: Number Attending:

Gift: Thank-You Sent:

Name & Address:

Phone: Number Attending:

Gift: Thank-You Sent:

Name & Address:

Phone: Number Attending:

Gift: Thank-You Sent:

Name & Address:

Phone: Number Attending:

Gift: Thank-You Sent:

Name & Address: | Phone: | Number Attending:
Gift: | Thank-You Sent:

Name & Address:
Phone: | Number Attending:
Gift: | Thank-You Sent:

Name & Address:
Phone: | Number Attending:
Gift: | Thank-You Sent:

Name & Address:
Phone: | Number Attending:
Gift: | Thank-You Sent:

Name & Address:
Phone: | Number Attending:
Gift: | Thank-You Sent:

Name & Address:
Phone: | Number Attending:
Gift: | Thank-You Sent:

Name & Address:
Phone: | Number Attending:
Gift: | Thank-You Sent:

Name & Address:
Phone: | Number Attending:
Gift: | Thank-You Sent:

Name & Address:
Phone: | Number Attending:
Gift: | Thank-You Sent:

Name & Address:

Phone: Number Attending:

Gift: Thank-You Sent:

Name & Address:

Phone: Number Attending:

Gift: Thank-You Sent:

Name & Address:

Phone: Number Attending:

Gift: Thank-You Sent:

Name & Address:

Phone: Number Attending:

Gift: Thank-You Sent:

Name & Address:

Phone: Number Attending:

Gift: Thank-You Sent:

Name & Address:

Phone: Number Attending:

Gift: Thank-You Sent:

Name & Address:

Phone: Number Attending:

Gift: Thank-You Sent:

Name & Address:

Phone: Number Attending:

Gift: Thank-You Sent:

Name & Address:

Phone: Number Attending:

Gift: Thank-You Sent:

Name & Address:

Phone: Number Attending:

Gift: Thank-You Sent:

Name & Address:	
Phone:	Number Attending:
Gift:	Thank-You Sent:
Name & Address:	
Phone:	Number Attending:
Gift:	Thank-You Sent:
Name & Address:	
Phone:	Number Attending:
Gift:	Thank-You Sent:
Name & Address:	
Phone:	Number Attending:
Gift:	Thank-You Sent:
Name & Address:	
Phone:	Number Attending:
Gift:	Thank-You Sent:
Name & Address:	
Phone:	Number Attending:
Gift:	Thank-You Sent:
Name & Address:	
Phone:	Number Attending:
Gift:	Thank-You Sent:
Name & Address:	
Phone:	Number Attending:
Gift:	Thank-You Sent:
Name & Address:	
Phone:	Number Attending:
Gift:	Thank-You Sent:

Name & Address:

Phone: .... Number Attending: ....

Gift: .... Thank-You Sent: ....

Name & Address:

Phone: .... Number Attending: ....

Gift: .... Thank-You Sent: ....

Name & Address:

Phone: .... Number Attending: ....

Gift: .... Thank-You Sent: ....

Name & Address:

Phone: .... Number Attending: ....

Gift: .... Thank-You Sent: ....

Name & Address:

Phone: .... Number Attending: ....

Gift: .... Thank-You Sent: ....

Name & Address:

Phone: .... Number Attending: ....

Gift: .... Thank-You Sent: ....

Name & Address:

Phone: .... Number Attending: ....

Gift: .... Thank-You Sent: ....

Name & Address:

Phone: .... Number Attending: ....

Gift: .... Thank-You Sent: ....

Name & Address:

Phone: .... Number Attending: ....

Gift: .... Thank-You Sent: ....

Name & Address:
....
Phone: .... Number Attending: ....
Gift: .... Thank-You Sent: ....

Name & Address:
....
Phone: .... Number Attending: ....
Gift: .... Thank-You Sent: ....

Name & Address:
....
Phone: .... Number Attending: ....
Gift: .... Thank-You Sent: ....

Name & Address:
....
Phone: .... Number Attending: ....
Gift: .... Thank-You Sent: ....

Name & Address:
....
Phone: .... Number Attending: ....
Gift: .... Thank-You Sent: ....

Name & Address:
....
Phone: .... Number Attending: ....
Gift: .... Thank-You Sent: ....

Name & Address:
....
Phone: .... Number Attending: ....
Gift: .... Thank-You Sent: ....

Name & Address:
....
Phone: .... Number Attending: ....
Gift: .... Thank-You Sent: ....

Name & Address:
....
Phone: .... Number Attending: ....
Gift: .... Thank-You Sent: ....

Name & Address:

Phone: Number Attending:

Gift: Thank-You Sent:

Name & Address:

Phone: Number Attending:

Gift: Thank-You Sent:

Name & Address:

Phone: Number Attending:

Gift: Thank-You Sent:

Name & Address:

Phone: Number Attending:

Gift: Thank-You Sent:

Name & Address:

Phone: Number Attending:

Gift: Thank-You Sent:

Name & Address:

Phone: Number Attending:

Gift: Thank-You Sent:

Name & Address:

Phone: Number Attending:

Gift: Thank-You Sent:

Name & Address:

Phone: Number Attending:

Gift: Thank-You Sent:

Name & Address:

Phone: Number Attending:

Gift: Thank-You Sent:

Name & Address:

Phone: Number Attending:

Gift: Thank-You Sent:

Name & Address:	
Phone:	Number Attending:
Gift:	Thank-You Sent:
Name & Address:	
Phone:	Number Attending:
Gift:	Thank-You Sent:
Name & Address:	
Phone:	Number Attending:
Gift:	Thank-You Sent:
Name & Address:	
Phone:	Number Attending:
Gift:	Thank-You Sent:
Name & Address:	
Phone:	Number Attending:
Gift:	Thank-You Sent:
Name & Address:	
Phone:	Number Attending:
Gift:	Thank-You Sent:
Name & Address:	
Phone:	Number Attending:
Gift:	Thank-You Sent:
Name & Address:	
Phone:	Number Attending:
Gift:	Thank-You Sent:
Name & Address:	
Phone:	Number Attending:
Gift:	Thank-You Sent:

Details

TASKS TO REMEMBER

Legal Name Change:
....
....

Newspaper Announcement:
....
....

Bride's Blood Test & Physical Exam:
....
....

Groom's Blood Test & Physical Exam:
....
....

Marriage License:
....
....

Other:
....
....
....
....
....
....
....

Details

LODGING FOR OUT-OF-TOWN GUESTS

Hotel:

Contact: Phone:

Rates: Reservations Made:

Guests: Dates Needed:

Guests: Dates Needed:

Guests: Dates Needed:

Guests: Dates Needed:

Guests: Dates Needed:

Guests: Dates Needed:

Guests: Dates Needed:

Guests: Dates Needed:

Guests: Dates Needed:

Guests: Dates Needed:

TRANSPORTATION ARRANGEMENTS

Parties, Showers & Gifts

Parties, Showers & Gifts

Sweet Anticipation
WEDDING REHEARSAL

Location:

Rehearsal Date: Time:

People Attending:

What to Rehearse:

Transportation:

In Celebration
REHEARSAL DINNER

Location:

Hosted by: Date: Time:

Guests:

Menu & Beverages:

Decorations & Details:

It has been said that love

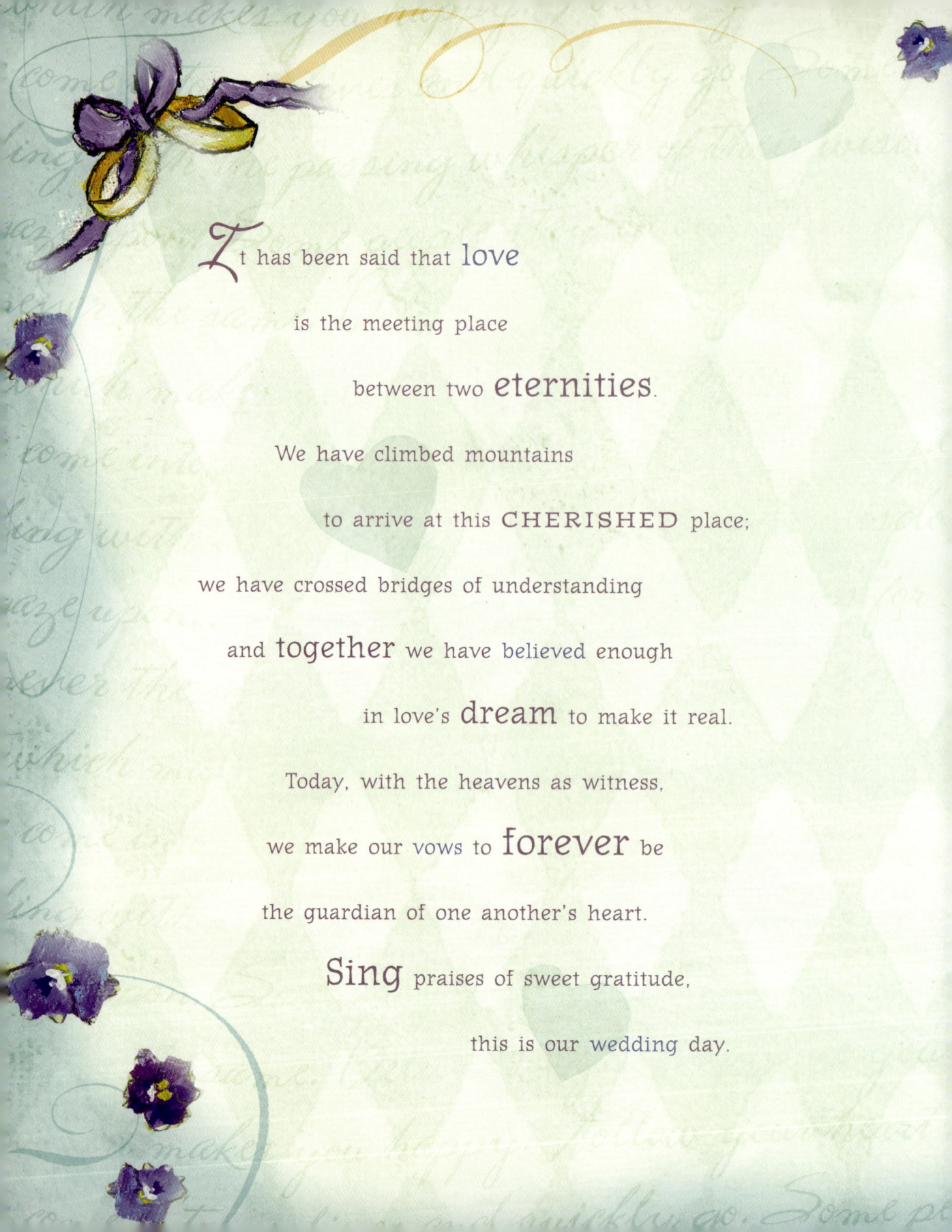

is the meeting place

between two eternities.

We have climbed mountains

to arrive at this CHERISHED place;

we have crossed bridges of understanding

and together we have believed enough

in love's dream to make it real.

Today, with the heavens as witness,

we make our vows to forever be

the guardian of one another's heart.

Sing praises of sweet gratitude,

this is our wedding day.

I Thee Wed

Time For Me

Hair & Manicure Appointments

Facial, Massage and Other Beauty Treatments

Private Moments

What I Feel Inside

What My Heart Tells Me

Loving Thoughts

Gift for Groom

A Note to My Love

Gifts of Heart

Gifts for Bridesmaids, Attendants & Family

Special Notes to Family & Loved Ones

The Eve of Bliss

8:00 A.M. _____

9:00 A.M. _____

10:00 A.M. _____

11:00 A.M. _____

12:00 P.M. _____

1:00 P.M. _____

2:00 P.M. _____

3:00 P.M. _____

4:00 P.M. _____

5:00 P.M. _____

6:00 P.M. _____

7:00 P.M. _____

8:00 P.M. _____

9:00 P.M. _____

10:00 P.M. _____

11:00 P.M. _____

12:00 A.M. _____

Our Wedding Day

8:00 A.M.

9:00 A.M.

10:00 A.M.

11:00 A.M.

12:00 P.M.

1:00 P.M.

2:00 P.M.

3:00 P.M.

4:00 P.M.

5:00 P.M.

6:00 P.M.

7:00 P.M.

8:00 P.M.

9:00 P.M.

10:00 P.M.

11:00 P.M.

12:00 A.M.

Bride's & Groom's Recollections

Forever and Always

Cherished Memories

Souvenirs of the Heart

Now that we've danced

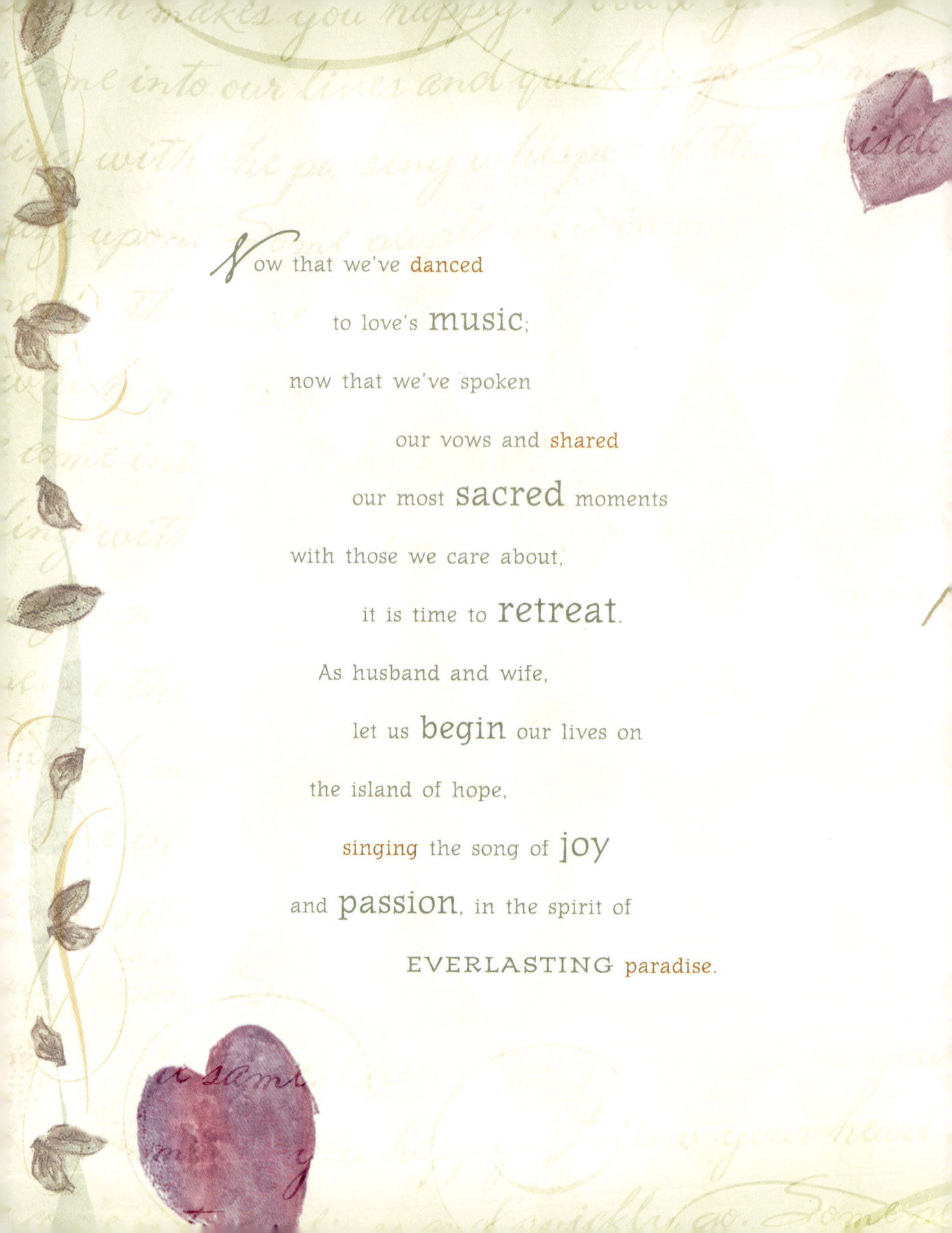

to love's music;

now that we've spoken

our vows and shared

our most sacred moments

with those we care about,

it is time to retreat.

As husband and wife,

let us begin our lives on

the island of hope,

singing the song of joy

and passion, in the spirit of

EVERLASTING paradise.

Paradise Found

The Honeymoon

TRAVEL AGENT

Contact: .... Phone: ....

Tickets: .... Passports: ....

Cost: .... Deposit Required: ....

ITINERARY

Location: .... Arrival: .... Departure: ....

Location: .... Arrival: .... Departure: ....

Location: .... Arrival: .... Departure: ....

Location: .... Arrival: .... Departure: ....

Special Plans / Notes:
....
....
....
....
....

On Our Way

ACCOMPANIONS

Location:

Hotel:

Contact: Phone:

Reservation Confirmation: Daily Rate:

Special Arrangements:

Transportation:

Location:

Hotel:

Contact: Phone:

Reservation Confirmation: Daily Rate:

Special Arrangements:

Transportation:

His and Hers

What to Pack

Don't Forget

Last Minute Details

Remembrances

And Keepsakes

Flavia

Lisa and her daughter Sylvie

    Flavia Weedn is one of America's leading contemporary inspirational writers and illustrators. Offering hope for the human spirit, Flavia portrays the basic excitement, simplicity and beauty she sees in the ordinary things of life. Her work has touched the lives of millions for over three decades.

    Lisa Weedn, Flavia's daughter and co-author, shares her mother's philosophy and passion. For over fifteen years, Lisa's writings have been a quiet messenger of the fundamental truth that age has no barrier on feelings of the human heart.

    Their collaborative work, which celebrates life and embraces meaningful core values, can be found in numerous books, collections of fine stationery goods, giftware, and lifestyle products distributed worldwide.

    Flavia and Lisa live in Santa Barbara, California.

Photos by Chris Chandler

which makes you happy.
come into our lives and quickly go. Some
ing with the passing whisper of their wisd
aze upon. Some people
ever the same.
which makes you happy. Follow your heart
and quickly go. Some pe